WE FLASH THEM, WE SMASH THEM,
WE PUSH THEM WAY UP,
WE SHAKE THEM, WE STUFF THEM
IN THE WRONG SIZED CUP,
OUR HUSBANDS JUST CRAVE THEM,
OUR CHILDREN HAVE DRAINED THEM,
SOME OF US EVEN DECIDED TO NAME THEM,
WE GO THROUGH OUR LIVES
AND KNOCK THEM ABOUT,
BUT ONE THING IS CERTAIN
ONE THING WE MUST SHOUT,
OUR BOOBIES HAVE BEEN THERE
THROUGH THICK AND THROUGH THIN,
AND LIFE IS TOO PRECIOUS
TO LET CANCER WIN!
LET'S FIND THE CURE!

YOU
GOT
THIS

Breast cancer found it's way in to my life
some time ago when my daughter's
grandmother was stricken twice within
a few years. I watched her go through
many painful challenges and changes
and she survived. I learned so much about
the disease and myself through her battle.
I wanted to help, I wanted so badly to be
able to do something that would make a
difference in the ongoing struggle with
this horrific disease. I found a way through
my creativity. I began to design a line of
greeting cards that would help spread
inspiration, hope and awareness. Some
of those designs are featured in this book.
My experience in designing those greeting
cards brought me into contact with so
many people who have been affected by
this disease either directly or indirectly.
I have been moved so deeply by so many
who have shared their stories with me,
each so much inspiring me in my endeavor.
Not long ago I learned that my daughter
and her mother both carry a form of
the "breast cancer gene" which has even
further motivated my desire to help in the
fight for survival and awareness. I have
conceived this book wishing to give some
smiles and hope with art, humor and heart
to those facing breast cancer

CONSIDER
YOURSELF
HUGGED

LOOK TO YOUR HEART
AND YOUR STRENGTH
WILL ASTOUND YOU,
YOUR PRAYERS WILL
BE ANSWERED
AND PEACE WILL
SURROUND YOU,
YOU MUST DRY YOUR EYES
FOR THE FUTURE AWAITS,
WITH PATIENCE AND COURAGE
SURVIVAL'S YOUR FATE

THE STEPS TO SURVIVAL START WITH YOU...
IT'S TIME TO SLIP ON YOUR SURVIVAL SHOES!

THE JOURNEY A BUTTERFLY

TAKES TO FIRST FLIGHT

IS MUCH LIKE A

CANCER SURVIVOR'S LONG FIGHT,

WITH COURAGE, CONVICTION,

PATIENCE AND HEART

YOUR JOURNEY TO BUTTERFLY

IS DESTINED TO START

THE FUTURE'S UNKNOWN,
WE CAN ONLY HAVE FAITH,
A HOPE THAT WE'RE BLESSED
EVERY DAY WHEN WE WAKE,
SO LOOK TO THE FUTURE
WITH A HEART FULL OF DREAMS,
YOUR DESTINY'S WHAT
YOU DESIGN IT TO BE!

LAUGH AT THE PAIN, DON'T BE DOWN IN A STUPOR... ON LIFE'S HARDEST DAYS FACE THE STRUGGLE WITH HUMOR!
SMILE

THERE'S
A
POWERFUL
FORCE
NO STORM
CAN UNDO,
THIS FORCE
BEYOND
MEASURE
IS SIMPLY
CALL
"YOU"

It's scary as hell when they say breast cancer,
On this party called life it can sure be a damper,
Some lose a breast some lose two,
The hair loss sucks and the meds make us puke,
But with ease we love men and our bodies give birth,
If we can handle that ladies we can deal with much worse!
Keep survival in sight, be courageous and patient,
After the storm comes a life
Celebration!

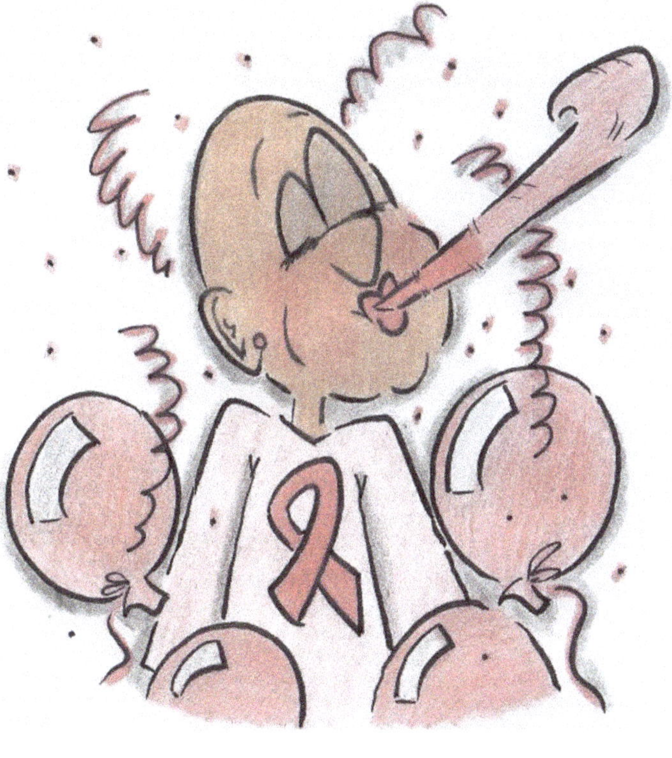

Be still and you'll hear it,
It's the sound of your spirit,
It will guide you
Don't fear it,

Survival's your fate,
Rejoice as you near it!

Share the Celebration

We've shared our minds,
We've shared our hearts,
We've shared this journey
with strength from the start,
We now share this prayer
thanking God
for our fate,
Hand in hand we've survived,
now we "must"
Celebrate!

"PINK" THE MAGIC DRAGON

Celebrate sexy, celebrate smarts,
celebrate laughter, celebrate heart,
Celebrate hope
and conquered fears,
Celebrate courage
and the many shed tears,
Celebrate change, celebrate faith,
Celebrate finding that
deep peaceful place,
Celebrate victory over this rival,
Celebrate family, friends
and survival

DON'T WASTE YOUR TIME
SIMPLY GRAZING ON MOODS,
DRY THOSE TEARS,
FIND YOUR SMILE
AND GET ON THE
MOOOOOOVE!

AT THE END OF
YOUR ROPE
AND YOU THINK
YOU CAN'T COPE?
KICK CANCER'S BUTT
WITH A BIG DOSE
OF HOPE!

NO MATTER THE
ERA FROM WHICH
YOU DERIVE,
LIVE AND
LOVE LIFE,
PAIN'S
JUST
CHANGE
IN
DISGUISE

Birthdays

I'm hoping your birthday
is second to none,
A day filled with laughter,
surprises and fun,
Our birthday's a time
when we celebrate life,
From humble beginnings,
through triumph and strife,
Your's is a life
I respect and admire,
You're a wonderful woman,
a friend and survivor!
HAPPY BIRTHDAY!

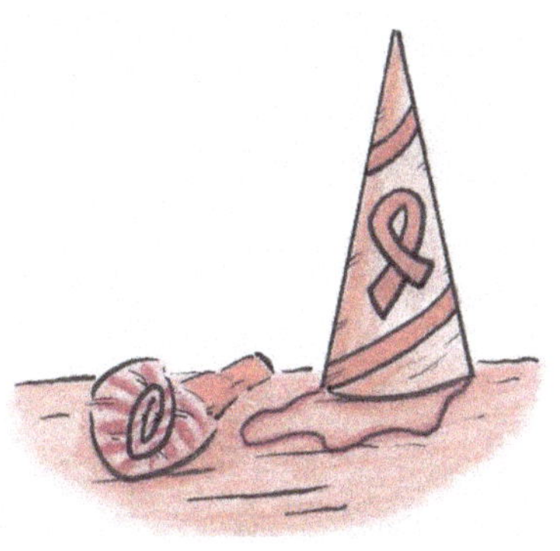

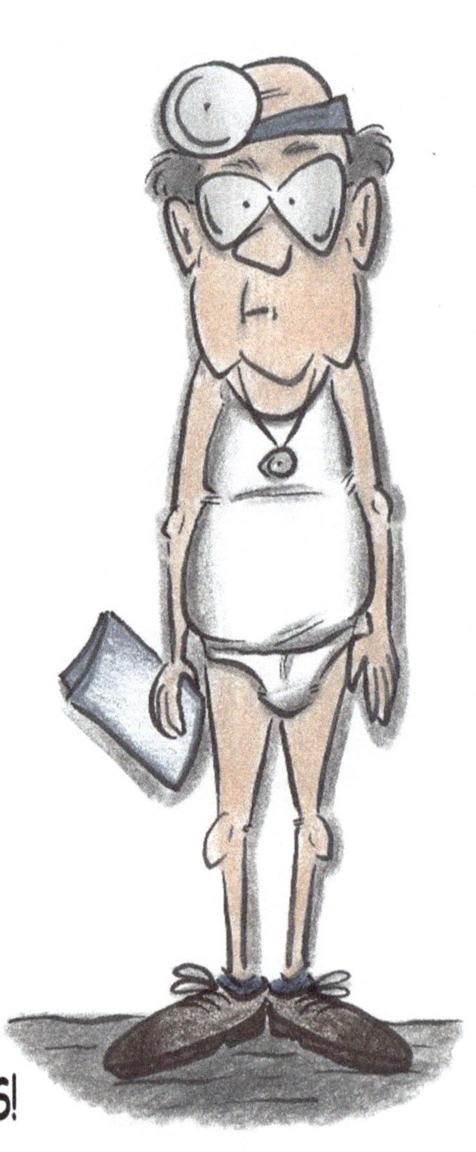

CHEMO"THERAPY"?
WHAT WERE
THEY THINKIN'?
IT'S NOT
THERAPEUTIC
UNLESS YOU'VE
BEEN DRINKIN'!
JUST THINK
FUNNY THOUGHTS
AND
GET WELL SOON,
TRY TO PICTURE
THE DOC IN HIS
FRUIT OF THE LOOMS!

When you're feeling down
and a smile can't be found,
Just know in your heart
there are angels
around!

DON'T BE AFRAID
YOU ARE PART OF GOD'S PLAN,
YOU'VE BEEN CHOSEN TO FIGHT
FOR HE KNOWS THAT YOU CAN,
HOLD ON TO HIS HAND
HE WILL HELP LEAD THE WAY,
TAKE COMFORT IN KNOWING
HE'S BESIDE YOU EACH DAY!

There's a train
to the future
that's ready
to move,
You've got
reservations
so banish
those blues!

Girlfriends

A SELFLESS HEART
AND AN EAGER SMILE,
I ASKED FOR AN INCH
AND SHE GAVE ME A MILE,
I NEEDED A SHOULDER
SHE OPENED HER ARMS,
I NEEDED A LAUGH
AND SHE TURNED ON THE CHARM,
I FEARED TILL THE END
I'D NOT MAKE IT ALIVE,
IF IT WASN'T FOR HER
I WOULD NOT HAVE SURVIVED,
SHE'S BROUGHT TO MY LIFE
A FRIENDSHIP SO TRUE,
THIS PAL, THIS BUDDY,
THIS GIRLFRIEND
IS YOU!

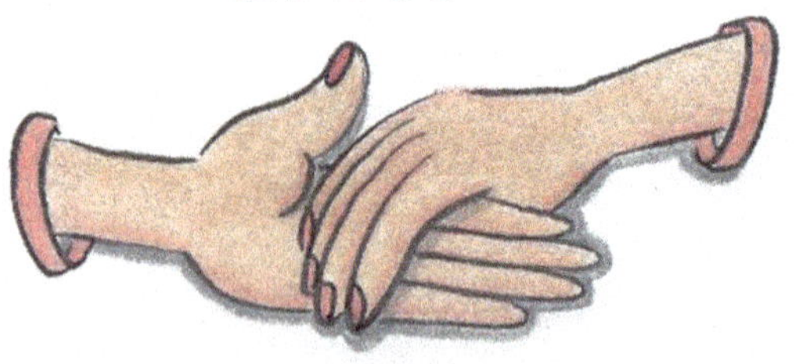

LOVE WHO YOU ARE,
CONQUER YOUR FEARS,
SURVIVE!
LIVE THE MOMENTS
DON'T COUNT THE YEARS,

GOD WILL NOT GIVE
WHAT OUR STRENGTH
WON'T ALLOW,
WITH COURAGE AND PRAYER
YOU WILL MAKE IT
SOME HOW

WITH OR WITHOUT'EM WE'VE STILL GOTTA SHOUT, BOOBS ARE WORTH HAVING BUT THERE'S MORE IT'S ABOUT! IT'S DIGNITY, WOMANHOOD, LIFE AND THE FIGHT, SO FIGHT FOR SURVIVAL WITH ALL OF YOUR MIGHT!!!!
GOT PINK?

*Survival won't come
from ribbons
alone,
Add some prayer
to your pink,
and your path will
be shown*

WHEN THE SKIES ARE GRAY
AND YOU'RE FEELING BLUE,
SLAP ON A SMILE,
LET YOUR PINK SIDE
SHINE THROUGH!

IN GOD WE FIND STRENGTH
AND A WILL TO SURVIVE,
WITH PRAYER THERE IS HOPE
WE'LL CONTINUE TO THRIVE,
HIS LOVE LETS US KNOW
THAT WE'RE ALWAYS FORGIVEN,
MY FAITH MAKES ME THINK
THAT HE WEARS A
PINK RIBBON!

The courage to fight
and the will to survive,
patience, hope
and a yearning to thrive,
It's all within reach,
the answers are there,
they're the keys
to survival,
and they lie within
prayer

SURVIVE!

A MOTHER'S WARM TOUCH,
A SISTER'S KIND WORDS,
A DAUGHTER'S SWEET SMILE
MEAN PRAYERS HAVE BEEN HEARD,
SIMPLE SWEET NOTHINGS
CAN QUIET YOUR FEARS,
THERE ARE ANGELS AMONG US
TO HELP DRY OUR TEARS,
SO CHERISH SMALL PLEASURES
THEIR LIGHT MAKES US STRONG
AND THE ROAD TO SURVIVAL
WON'T SEEM QUITE AS LONG

Miracles happen,
Wishes come true,
With faith you will find
the survivor in you!

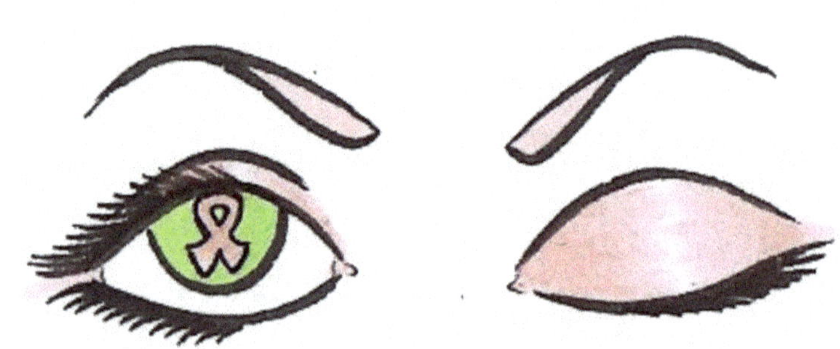

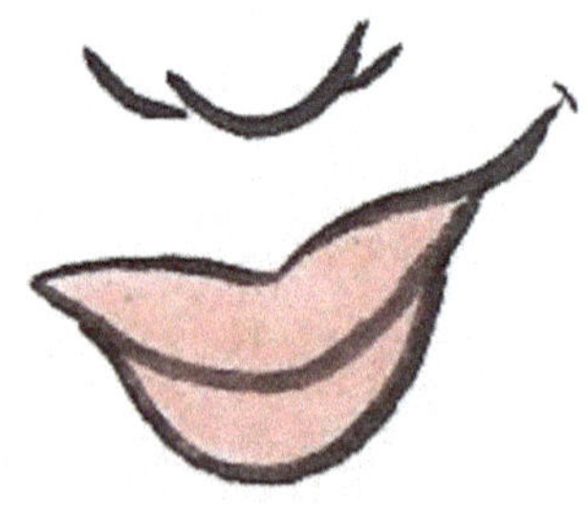

It's okay to cry
but in time dry your eyes,
It's okay to scream
but hang on to your dreams,
It's okay to fear
when the future's unclear, 
And it's okay
to smile,
You'll survive this
with style!

DON'T GIVE UP, DON'T GIVE IN, SURVIVAL STARTS WHEN THE BATTLE BEGINS!

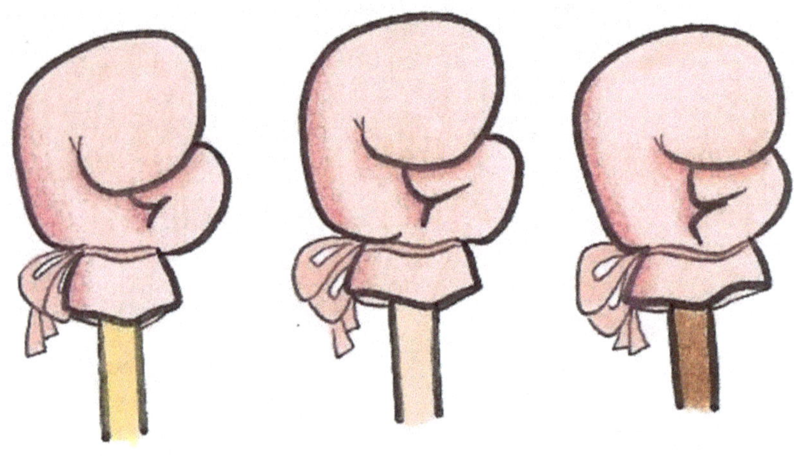

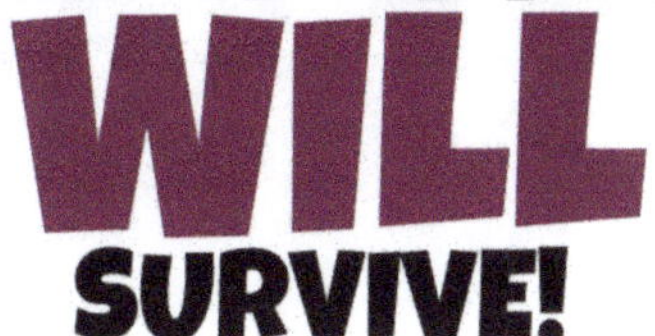
SURVIVE!
THINK ABOUT STRENGTH,
LET YOUR SPIRIT
TAKE FLIGHT...
THINK OF YOUR DREAMS
AND HOW YOU
WILL
SURVIVE!

THERE'S NO PLACE LIKE SURVIVAL,
THERE'S NO PLACE LIKE SURVIVAL,

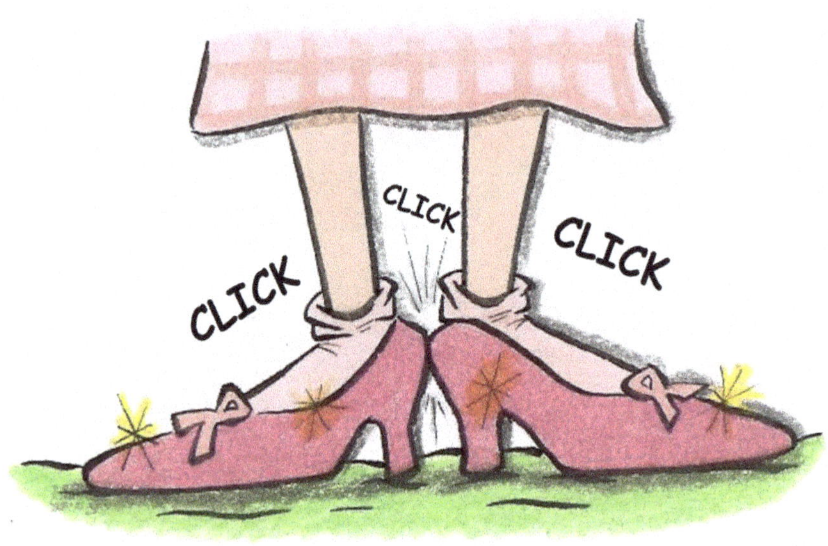

THERE'S NO PLACE LIKE SURVIVAL!

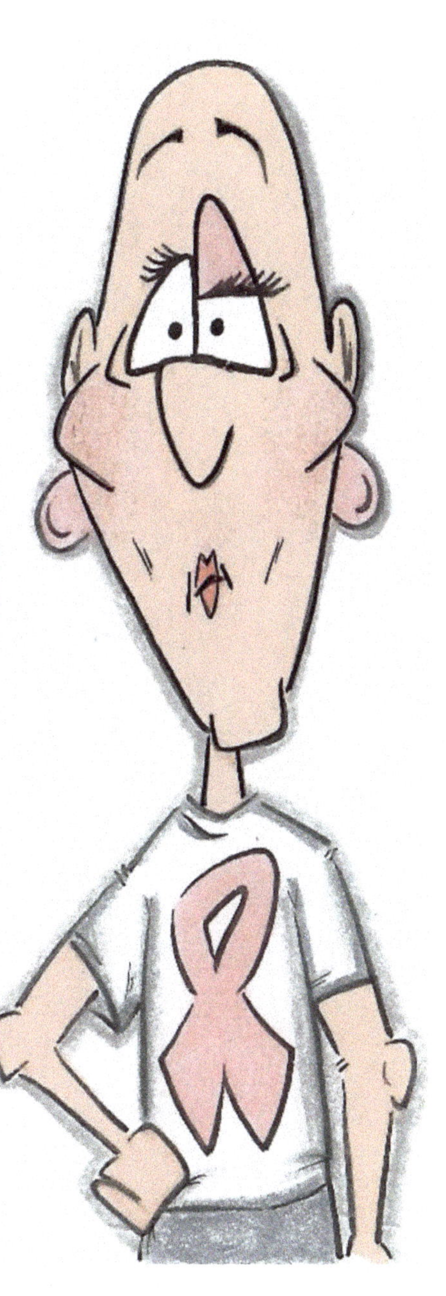

LOOK AT
IT
THIS WAY,
IT COULD BE
MUCH WORSE!
IT'S ONLY
CHEMO,
YOU AIN'T
LOST
YOUR PURSE!

Look to your heart
and your strength
will astound you,
Your prayers will
be answered
and peace will
surround you,
You must dry your eyes
for the future awaits,
With patience and courage
survival's your fate

CANCER WON'T BEAT US,
IT WON'T TAKE OUR SMILE,
NOT TO MENTION THE FACT
WE BROUGHT WIGS BACK IN STYLE!

With selfless devotion
you're courageous and kind,
the love that you share
seems so easy to find,
I love and respect you
from now 'til the end,
You are woman,
survivor, mother
and friend

BREAST CANCER BRINGS ABOUT ALL KINDS OF TROUBLES, BUT DON'T LET THE STRIFE OF YOUR FIGHT BURST YOUR BUBBLE!

NEVER UNDERESTIMATE THE POWER OF PINK!

JUMP IN THE RING AND PREPARE TO FIGHT, ONE REASON, ONE PURPOSE, ONE VISION IN SIGHT, WE GOTTA BE QUICK WE GOTTA BE FAST, THE TIME HAS ARRIVED TO KICK BREAST CANCER'S ASS!!!

THE HOLIDAY SEASON
CAN REALLY BE
DRAINING,
BUT I'M BLESSED
AND ALIVE AND I
AIN'T COMPLAINING,
NOT LONG AGO
THOUGHT I'D SEEN
MY LAST
CHRISTMAS,
BUT I'M A SURVIVOR
AND NOW BACK
IN BUSINESS,
SO LET'S NOT LET
HOLIDAY STRESS
GET US DOWN,
THANK GOD
FOR THE SEASON
AND THAT WE'RE
STILL AROUND!

BREAST CANCER CHANGES
YOUR LIFE OVERNIGHT,
HOLD TIGHT TO YOUR
DREAMS AND KEEP THE
FUTURE IN SIGHT,
DON'T LET YOUR FEAR
OR YOUR TEARS CLOUD
YOUR VISION,
REACH DEEP INSIDE
AND SEE IT'S ALL
A TRANSITION.

CANCER WILL
CHALLENGE BOTH
BODY AND SOUL,
THE DESTRUCTION
AND SCARS MAKE
YOU FEEL LESS
THAN WHOLE,
BUT GOD DOESN'T
LEAVE US TO
BATTLE ALONE,
OUR PRAYERS ARE
THE THREAD OF
WHICH MIRACLES
ARE SEWN,
YOUR PRAYERS WILL
BE TAKEN TO GOD
AND BE GIVEN,
AND THE ANGELS
THAT TAKE THEM
ARE WEARING
PINK RIBBONS!

THROUGHOUT
OUR BATTLE
WE ALL MUST
REMEMBER,
BREAST CANCER
TOUCHES EACH
FAMILY MEMBER,
THE ANGER, THE
SADNESS AND
QUESTIONS OF
WHY,
BUT STRENGTH
BEYOND MEASURE
LIES WITHIN
FAMILY TIES,
SO SHARE ALL
THE ANGER,
THE FEAR AND
THE PAIN,
TOGETHERNESS
SHIELDS THROUGH
BREAST CANCER'S
RAIN!

ROSES ARE RED AND
VIOLETS ARE BLUE,
I NOW HAVE ONE
WHERE THERE USED
TO BE TWO,
BUT I'M STILL ALL
WOMAN INSIDE AND OUT,
A MOVER A SHAKER WHO
WON'T SIT AND POUT,
THE BATTLE AIN'T EASY
SOME DAYS ARE ROUGH,
BUT YOU GOTTA BE STRONG
YOU GOTTA BE TOUGH,
SO AS I MOVE ON AND
CELEBRATE LIFE,
I MUST SHARE MY STORY
TO HELP OTHERS SURVIVE!

HANG IN THERE!

BREAST CANCER'S WRATH CAN SURELY BE TRAGIC, BUT PRAY AND HANG TOUGH FOR YOUR STRENGTH CAN WORK MAGIC, IT WON'T BE AS EASY AS RUBBING A LAMP, BUT FIGHT FOR YOUR LIFE AND YOU'LL COME OUT A CHAMP!

BREAST CANCER SUCKS BUT WE MUST STAND TALL,
ALL FOR ONE AND ONE FOR ALL,
LET'S FIGHT FOR SURVIVAL LET'S HUNT DOWN THE CURE,
BE BRAVE AND REMEMBER THAT ONE THING'S FOR SURE,
LIFE IS NOT OVER IT'S SIMPLY JUST STALLED,
AND WE STILL LOOK DAMN GOOD THOUGH OUR HEADS ARE NOW BALD!!
MS PINK RIBBON AMERICA

BREAST CANCER CHANGES YOUR LIFE OVERNIGHT, HOLD TIGHT TO YOUR DREAMS AND KEEP THE FUTURE IN SIGHT, DON'T LET YOUR FEAR OR YOUR TEARS CLOUD YOUR VISION, REACH DEEP INSIDE AND SEE IT'S ALL A TRANSITION.

RECOVERY STARTS IN YOUR MIND AND YOUR SPIRIT, WE MUSTN'T LET BREAST CANCER KNOW THAT WE FEAR IT, STAND AND BE STRONG AND CRY IF YOU MUST, BUT NOW IS THE TIME IN YOURSELF YOU MUST TRUST!

When your hope's gone adrift
and you're drowning in tears,
reach for the pink, it will help calm
your fears

BREAST CANCER
BRINGS ON A
LOOK ALL IT'S OWN,
MY BOOB'S GONE,
MY HAIR'S GONE,
I'M THIN AS
AS A BONE,
BUT BEAUTY'S
NOT BOOBIES
OR LONG
FLOWING HAIR,
BEAUTY'S THE
KNOWLEDGE
AND COURAGE
I SHARE,
THE SURVIVOR
INSIDE ME,
THE WOMAN
I AM,
SO I MAY BE
BALD BUT I
DON'T GIVE
A DAMN!
SURVIVE

THE BATTLE
IS ON WITH
A TOUGH
OPPOSITION,
BUT HAND IN
HAND WE'LL
SURVIVE THIS
TRANSITION!

survive

TAKE A STEP,
DO NOT
FEAR...
YOU'LL
MAKE IT
THROUGH,
JUST
PERSEVERE

MORTALITY STRIKES
AND YOU'RE FILLED WITH FEAR,
THE ANGER, THE QUESTIONS,
CONFUSION AND TEARS...
DON'T LET IT BEAT YOU
IT'S TIME TO SWITCH GEARS,
RACE TO THE FINISH LINE
BRING ON THE CHEERS...
TAKE LIFE BY THE WHEEL,
TURN IT ON, HIT THE GAS,
SHOUT
"BREAST CANCER SUCKS
AND CAN KISS MY SWEET ASS"

CANCER SURVIVAL WILL
MAKE YOUR HEART SING,
AND THE PATH TO RECOVERY
WILL BRING YOU YOUR WINGS,
YOUR LIFE HAS BEEN ALTERED
IN SO MANY WAYS,
YOUR BODY, YOUR SPIRIT AND
EMOTIONS HAVE CHANGED,
AND JUST LIKE THE BUTTERFLY
TOUCHES EACH FLOWER,
YOU NOW MUST TOUCH OTHERS
FOR KNOWLEDGE IS POWER,
SO SPREAD YOUR WINGS
AND TOUCH THE SKY,
COURAGEOUS SURVIVOR,
TAKE FLIGHT BUTTERFLY!

EVEN IN MOMENTS THAT SEEM WAY TOO TOUGH

GIVE IT YOUR ALL AND DON'T EVER GIVE UP

STRIVE TO
SURVIVE
AND CHERISH
TODAY...
PINK RIBBONS
DON'T MEAN
THAT WE
SELL
MARY KAY!

THERE'S SOMEONE I KNOW
WHO I'D LIKE YOU TO MEET,
SHE'S COURAGEOUS AND WISE
WITH A FAITH THAT RUNS DEEP,
WITH HER SMILE AND HER STRENGTH
SHE WILL MAKE YOUR PATH CLEARER,
HER NAME IS SURVIVOR
AND SHE'S THERE IN YOUR MIRROR

WE FLASH THEM, WE SMASH THEM,
WE PUSH THEM WAY UP,
WE SHAKE THEM, WE STUFF THEM
IN THE WRONG SIZED CUP,
OUR HUSBANDS JUST CRAVE THEM,
OUR CHILDREN HAVE DRAINED THEM,
SOME OF US EVEN DECIDED TO NAME THEM,
WE GO THROUGH OUR LIVES
AND KNOCK THEM ABOUT,
BUT ONE THING IS CERTAIN
ONE THING WE MUST SHOUT,
OUR BOOBIES HAVE BEEN THERE
THROUGH THICK AND THROUGH THIN,
AND LIFE IS TOO PRECIOUS
TO LET CANCER WIN!
LET'S FIND THE CURE!

YOU
GOT
THIS

LOOK TO YOUR HEART
AND YOUR STRENGTH
WILL ASTOUND YOU,
YOUR PRAYERS WILL
BE ANSWERED
AND PEACE WILL
SURROUND YOU,
YOU MUST DRY YOUR EYES
FOR THE FUTURE AWAITS,
WITH PATIENCE AND COURAGE
SURVIVAL'S YOUR FATE

THE STEPS TO
SURVIVAL START
WITH YOU...
IT'S TIME TO
SLIP ON YOUR
SURVIVAL
SHOES!

THE JOURNEY A BUTTERFLY

TAKES TO FIRST FLIGHT

IS MUCH LIKE A

CANCER SURVIVOR'S LONG FIGHT,

WITH COURAGE, CONVICTION,

PATIENCE AND HEART

YOUR JOURNEY TO BUTTERFLY

IS DESTINED TO START

THE FUTURE'S UNKNOWN,
WE CAN ONLY HAVE FAITH,
A HOPE THAT WE'RE BLESSED
EVERY DAY WHEN WE WAKE,
SO LOOK TO THE FUTURE
WITH A HEART FULL OF DREAMS,
YOUR DESTINY'S WHAT
YOU DESIGN IT TO BE!

LAUGH AT THE PAIN, DON'T BE DOWN IN A STUPOR... ON LIFE'S HARDEST DAYS FACE THE STRUGGLE WITH HUMOR!
SMILE

THERE'S A POWERFUL FORCE NO STORM CAN UNDO, THIS FORCE BEYOND MEASURE IS SIMPLY CALL "YOU"

It's scary as hell when they say breast cancer,
On this party called life it can sure be a damper,
Some lose a breast some lose two,
The hair loss sucks and the meds make us puke,
But with ease we love men and our bodies give birth,
If we can handle that ladies we can deal with much worse!
Keep survival in sight, be courageous and patient,
After the storm comes a life
Celebration!

Be still and you'll hear it,
It's the sound of your spirit,
It will guide you
Don't fear it,

Survival's your fate,
Rejoice as you near it!

Share the Celebration

We've shared our minds,
We've shared our hearts,
We've shared this journey
with strength from the start,
We now share this prayer
thanking God
for our fate,
Hand in hand we've survived,
now we "must"
Celebrate!

"PINK" THE MAGIC DRAGON

Celebrate sexy, celebrate smarts,
celebrate laughter, celebrate heart,
Celebrate hope
and conquered fears,
Celebrate courage
and the many shed tears,
Celebrate change, celebrate faith,
Celebrate finding that
deep peaceful place,
Celebrate victory over this rival,
Celebrate family, friends
and survival

DON'T WASTE YOUR TIME
SIMPLY GRAZING ON MOODS,
DRY THOSE TEARS,
FIND YOUR SMILE
AND GET ON THE
MOOOOOOVE!

AT THE END OF
YOUR ROPE
AND YOU THINK
YOU CAN'T COPE?
KICK CANCER'S BUTT
WITH A BIG DOSE
OF HOPE!

NO MATTER THE
ERA FROM WHICH
YOU DERIVE,
LIVE AND
LOVE LIFE,
PAIN'S
JUST
CHANGE
IN
DISGUISE

Birthdays

I'm hoping your birthday
is second to none,
A day filled with laughter,
surprises and fun,
Our birthday's a time
when we celebrate life,
From humble beginnings,
through triumph and strife,
Your's is a life
I respect and admire,
You're a wonderful woman,
a friend and survivor!
HAPPY BIRTHDAY!

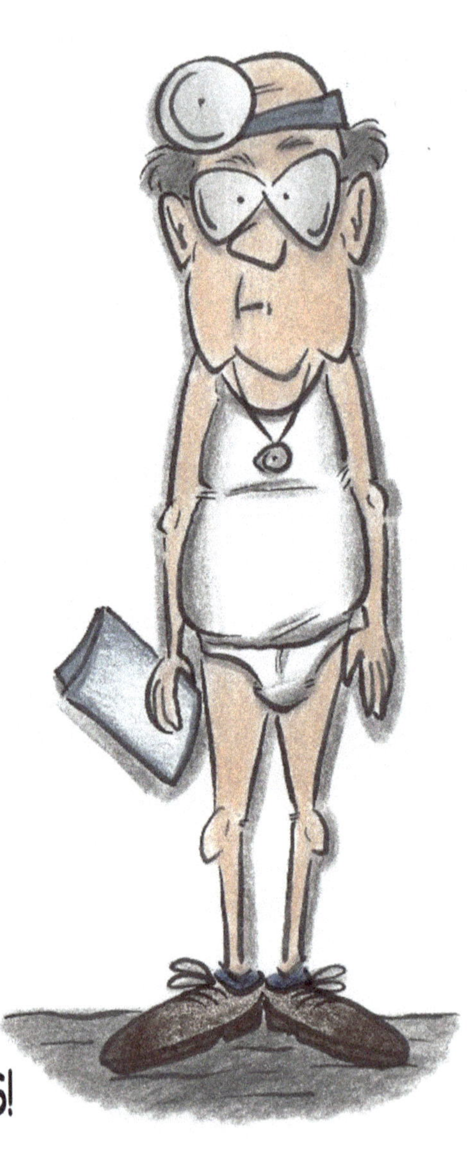

CHEMO"THERAPY"?
WHAT WERE
THEY THINKIN'?
IT'S NOT
THERAPEUTIC
UNLESS YOU'VE
BEEN DRINKIN'!
JUST THINK
FUNNY THOUGHTS
AND
GET WELL SOON,
TRY TO PICTURE
THE DOC IN HIS
FRUIT OF THE LOOMS!

When you're feeling down
and a smile can't be found,
Just know in your heart
there are angels
around!

DON'T BE AFRAID
YOU ARE PART OF GOD'S PLAN,
YOU'VE BEEN CHOSEN TO FIGHT
FOR HE KNOWS THAT YOU CAN,
HOLD ON TO HIS HAND
HE WILL HELP LEAD THE WAY,
TAKE COMFORT IN KNOWING
HE'S BESIDE YOU EACH DAY!

There's a train
to the future
that's ready
to move,
You've got
reservations
so banish
those blues!

Girlfriends

A SELFLESS HEART
AND AN EAGER SMILE,
I ASKED FOR AN INCH
AND SHE GAVE ME A MILE,
I NEEDED A SHOULDER
SHE OPENED HER ARMS,
I NEEDED A LAUGH
AND SHE TURNED ON THE CHARM,
I FEARED TILL THE END
I'D NOT MAKE IT ALIVE,
IF IT WASN'T FOR HER
I WOULD NOT HAVE SURVIVED,
SHE'S BROUGHT TO MY LIFE
A FRIENDSHIP SO TRUE,
THIS PAL, THIS BUDDY,
THIS GIRLFRIEND
IS YOU!

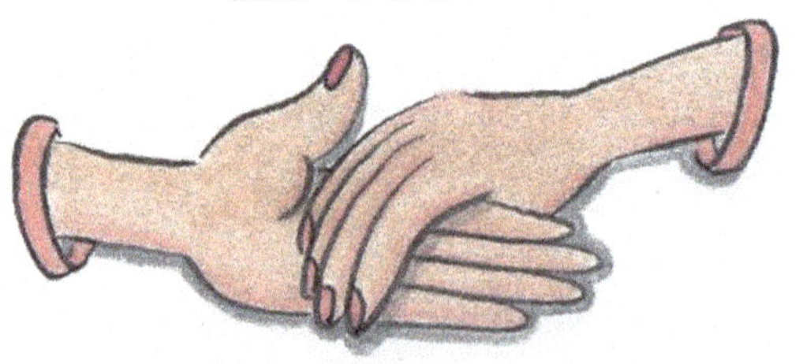

LOVE WHO YOU ARE,
CONQUER YOUR FEARS,
SURVIVE!
LIVE THE MOMENTS
DON'T COUNT THE YEARS,

GOD WILL NOT GIVE
WHAT OUR STRENGTH
WON'T ALLOW,
WITH COURAGE AND PRAYER
YOU WILL MAKE IT
SOME HOW

WITH OR WITHOUT'EM WE'VE STILL GOTTA SHOUT, BOOBS ARE WORTH HAVING BUT THERE'S MORE IT'S ABOUT! IT'S DIGNITY, WOMANHOOD, LIFE AND THE FIGHT, SO FIGHT FOR SURVIVAL WITH ALL OF YOUR MIGHT!!!!
GOT PINK?

*Survival won't come
from ribbons
alone,
Add some prayer
to your pink,
and your path will
be shown*

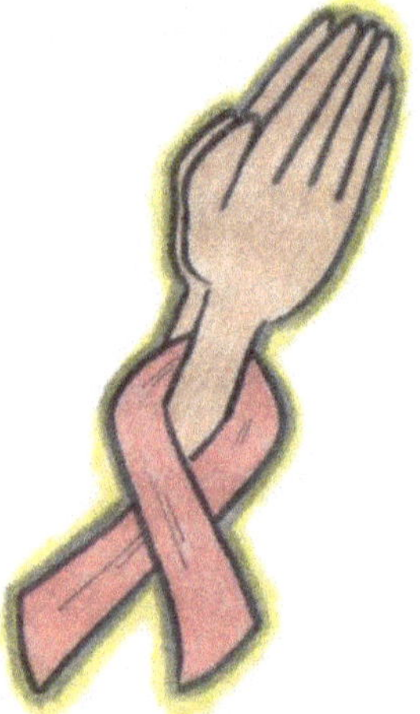

WHEN THE SKIES ARE GRAY
AND YOU'RE FEELING BLUE,
SLAP ON A SMILE,
LET YOUR PINK SIDE
SHINE THROUGH!

IN GOD WE FIND STRENGTH
AND A WILL TO SURVIVE,
WITH PRAYER THERE IS HOPE
WE'LL CONTINUE TO THRIVE,
HIS LOVE LETS US KNOW
THAT WE'RE ALWAYS FORGIVEN,
MY FAITH MAKES ME THINK
THAT HE WEARS A
PINK RIBBON!

The courage to fight
and the will to survive,
patience, hope
and a yearning to thrive,
It's all within reach,
the answers are there,
they're the keys
to survival,
and they lie within
prayer

SURVIVE!

A MOTHER'S WARM TOUCH,
A SISTER'S KIND WORDS,
A DAUGHTER'S SWEET SMILE
MEAN PRAYERS HAVE BEEN HEARD,
SIMPLE SWEET NOTHINGS
CAN QUIET YOUR FEARS,
THERE ARE ANGELS AMONG US
TO HELP DRY OUR TEARS,
SO CHERISH SMALL PLEASURES
THEIR LIGHT MAKES US STRONG
AND THE ROAD TO SURVIVAL
WON'T SEEM QUITE AS LONG

Miracles happen,
Wishes come true,
With faith you will find
the survivor in you!

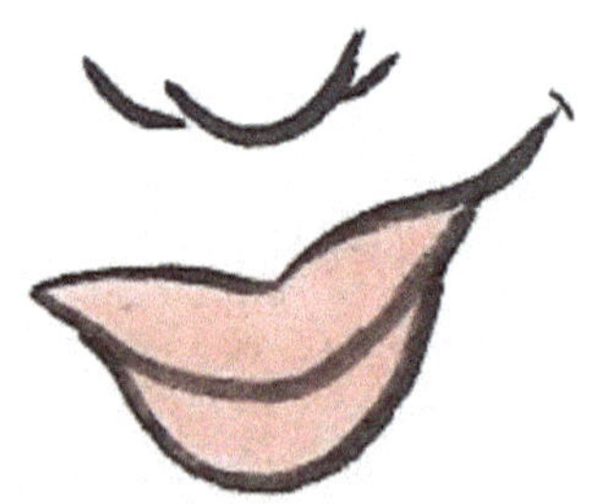

It's okay to cry
but in time dry your eyes,
It's okay to scream
but hang on to your dreams,
It's okay to fear
when the future's unclear,

And it's okay
to smile,
You'll survive this
with style!

DON'T GIVE UP, DON'T GIVE IN, SURVIVAL STARTS WHEN THE BATTLE BEGINS!

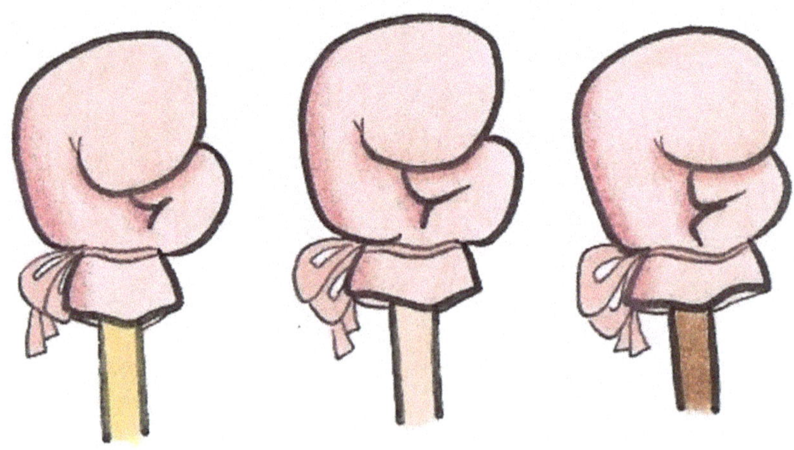

THINK ABOUT STRENGTH, LET YOUR SPIRIT TAKE FLIGHT... THINK OF YOUR DREAMS AND HOW YOU WILL SURVIVE!

THERE'S NO PLACE LIKE SURVIVAL,
THERE'S NO PLACE LIKE SURVIVAL,

THERE'S NO PLACE LIKE SURVIVAL!

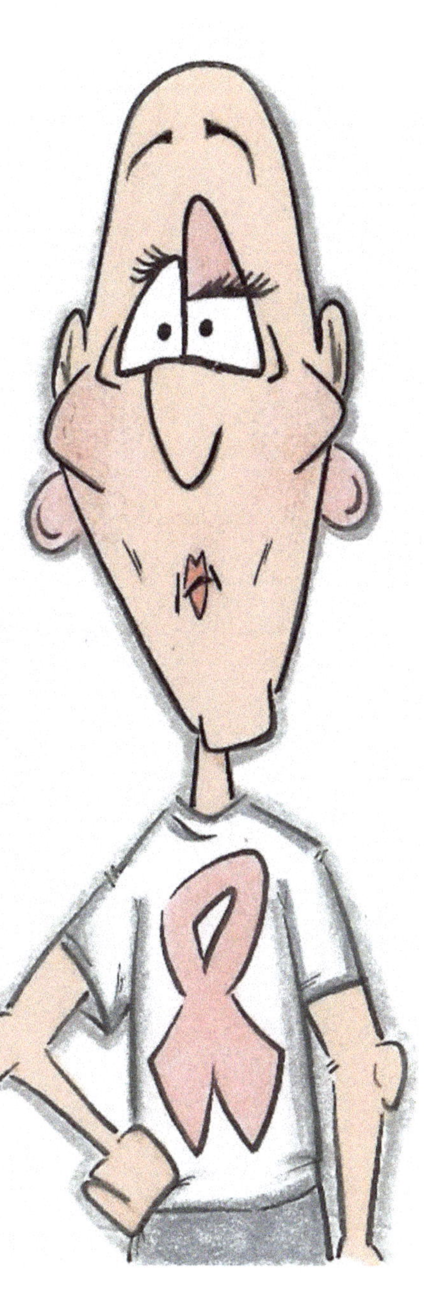

LOOK AT
IT
THIS WAY,
IT COULD BE
MUCH WORSE!
IT'S ONLY
CHEMO,
YOU AIN'T
LOST
YOUR PURSE!

Look to your heart
and your strength
will astound you,
Your prayers will
be answered
and peace will
surround you,
You must dry your eyes
for the future awaits,
With patience and courage
survival's your fate

CANCER WON'T BEAT US,
IT WON'T TAKE OUR SMILE,
NOT TO MENTION THE FACT
WE BROUGHT WIGS BACK IN STYLE!

With selfless devotion
you're courageous and kind,
the love that you share
seems so easy to find,
I love and respect you
from now 'til the end,
You are woman,
survivor, mother
and friend

BREAST CANCER BRINGS ABOUT
ALL KINDS OF TROUBLES,
BUT DON'T LET THE
STRIFE OF YOUR FIGHT
BURST YOUR BUBBLE!

NEVER UNDERESTIMATE THE POWER OF PINK!

JUMP IN THE RING AND PREPARE TO FIGHT,
ONE REASON, ONE PURPOSE, ONE VISION IN SIGHT,
WE GOTTA BE QUICK WE GOTTA BE FAST,
THE TIME HAS ARRIVED TO KICK BREAST CANCER'S ASS!!!

THE HOLIDAY SEASON
CAN REALLY BE
DRAINING,
BUT I'M BLESSED
AND ALIVE AND I
AIN'T COMPLAINING,
NOT LONG AGO
THOUGHT I'D SEEN
MY LAST
CHRISTMAS,
BUT I'M A SURVIVOR
AND NOW BACK
IN BUSINESS,
SO LET'S NOT LET
HOLIDAY STRESS
GET US DOWN,
THANK GOD
FOR THE SEASON
AND THAT WE'RE
STILL AROUND!

BREAST CANCER CHANGES
YOUR LIFE OVERNIGHT,
HOLD TIGHT TO YOUR
DREAMS AND KEEP THE
FUTURE IN SIGHT,
DON'T LET YOUR FEAR
OR YOUR TEARS CLOUD
YOUR VISION,
REACH DEEP INSIDE
AND SEE IT'S ALL
A TRANSITION.

CANCER WILL
CHALLENGE BOTH
BODY AND SOUL,
THE DESTRUCTION
AND SCARS MAKE
YOU FEEL LESS
THAN WHOLE,
BUT GOD DOESN'T
LEAVE US TO
BATTLE ALONE,
OUR PRAYERS ARE
THE THREAD OF
WHICH MIRACLES
ARE SEWN,
YOUR PRAYERS WILL
BE TAKEN TO GOD
AND BE GIVEN,
AND THE ANGELS
THAT TAKE THEM
ARE WEARING
PINK RIBBONS!

THROUGHOUT OUR BATTLE WE ALL MUST REMEMBER,
BREAST CANCER TOUCHES EACH FAMILY MEMBER,
THE ANGER, THE SADNESS AND QUESTIONS OF WHY,
BUT STRENGTH BEYOND MEASURE LIES WITHIN FAMILY TIES,
SO SHARE ALL THE ANGER, THE FEAR AND THE PAIN,
TOGETHERNESS SHIELDS THROUGH BREAST CANCER'S RAIN!

ROSES ARE RED AND
VIOLETS ARE BLUE,
I NOW HAVE ONE
WHERE THERE USED
TO BE TWO,
BUT I'M STILL ALL
WOMAN INSIDE AND OUT,
A MOVER A SHAKER WHO
WON'T SIT AND POUT,
THE BATTLE AIN'T EASY
SOME DAYS ARE ROUGH,
BUT YOU GOTTA BE STRONG
YOU GOTTA BE TOUGH,
SO AS I MOVE ON AND
CELEBRATE LIFE,
I MUST SHARE MY STORY
TO HELP OTHERS SURVIVE!

HANG IN THERE!

BREAST CANCER'S
WRATH CAN SURELY
BE TRAGIC,
BUT PRAY AND
HANG TOUGH
FOR YOUR STRENGTH
CAN WORK MAGIC,
IT WON'T BE AS
EASY AS
RUBBING A LAMP,
BUT FIGHT FOR
YOUR LIFE AND
YOU'LL COME
OUT A CHAMP!

BREAST CANCER SUCKS BUT WE MUST STAND TALL,
ALL FOR ONE AND ONE FOR ALL,
LET'S FIGHT FOR SURVIVAL
LET'S HUNT DOWN THE CURE,
BE BRAVE AND REMEMBER THAT ONE THING'S FOR SURE,
LIFE IS NOT OVER IT'S SIMPLY JUST STALLED,
AND WE STILL LOOK DAMN GOOD THOUGH OUR HEADS ARE NOW BALD!!
MS PINK RIBBON AMERICA

BREAST CANCER CHANGES YOUR LIFE OVERNIGHT, HOLD TIGHT TO YOUR DREAMS AND KEEP THE FUTURE IN SIGHT, DON'T LET YOUR FEAR OR YOUR TEARS CLOUD YOUR VISION, REACH DEEP INSIDE AND SEE IT'S ALL A TRANSITION.

RECOVERY STARTS
IN YOUR MIND
AND YOUR
SPIRIT,
WE MUSTN'T LET
BREAST CANCER
KNOW THAT WE
FEAR IT,
STAND AND BE
STRONG AND
CRY IF
YOU MUST,
BUT NOW IS
THE TIME
IN YOURSELF
YOU MUST TRUST!

When your hope's gone adrift
and you're drowning in tears,
reach for the pink, it will help calm
your fears

BREAST CANCER
BRINGS ON A
LOOK ALL IT'S OWN,
MY BOOB'S GONE,
MY HAIR'S GONE,
I'M THIN AS
AS A BONE,
BUT BEAUTY'S
NOT BOOBIES
OR LONG
FLOWING HAIR,
BEAUTY'S THE
KNOWLEDGE
AND COURAGE
I SHARE,
THE SURVIVOR
INSIDE ME,
THE WOMAN
I AM,
SO I MAY BE
BALD BUT I
DON'T GIVE
A DAMN!
SURVIVE

THE BATTLE
IS ON WITH
A TOUGH
OPPOSITION,
BUT HAND IN
HAND WE'LL
SURVIVE THIS
TRANSITION!
survive

TAKE A STEP,
DO NOT
FEAR...
YOU'LL
MAKE IT
THROUGH,
JUST
PERSEVERE

MORTALITY STRIKES
AND YOU'RE FILLED WITH FEAR,
THE ANGER, THE QUESTIONS,
CONFUSION AND TEARS...
DON'T LET IT BEAT YOU
IT'S TIME TO SWITCH GEARS,
RACE TO THE FINISH LINE
BRING ON THE CHEERS...
TAKE LIFE BY THE WHEEL,
TURN IT ON, HIT THE GAS,
SHOUT
"BREAST CANCER SUCKS
AND CAN KISS MY SWEET ASS"

CANCER SURVIVAL WILL
MAKE YOUR HEART SING,
AND THE PATH TO RECOVERY
WILL BRING YOU YOUR WINGS,
YOUR LIFE HAS BEEN ALTERED
IN SO MANY WAYS,
YOUR BODY, YOUR SPIRIT AND
EMOTIONS HAVE CHANGED,
AND JUST LIKE THE BUTTERFLY
TOUCHES EACH FLOWER,
YOU NOW MUST TOUCH OTHERS
FOR KNOWLEDGE IS POWER,
SO SPREAD YOUR WINGS
AND TOUCH THE SKY,
COURAGEOUS SURVIVOR,
TAKE FLIGHT BUTTERFLY!

EVEN IN MOMENTS THAT SEEM WAY TOO TOUGH

GIVE IT YOUR ALL AND DON'T EVER GIVE UP

STRIVE TO SURVIVE AND CHERISH TODAY... PINK RIBBONS DON'T MEAN THAT WE SELL MARY KAY!
October is Breast Cancer Awareness Month...
...know your body

THERE'S SOMEONE I KNOW
WHO I'D LIKE YOU TO MEET,
SHE'S COURAGEOUS AND WISE
WITH A FAITH THAT RUNS DEEP,
WITH HER SMILE AND HER STRENGTH
SHE WILL MAKE YOUR PATH CLEARER,
HER NAME IS SURVIVOR
AND SHE'S THERE IN YOUR MIRROR

SOME BOOBS ARE PERKY,
SOME BOOBS ARE BIG,
SOME BOOBS ARE TINY,
SOME SHAPED LIKE FIGS
AND SOME BOOBS ARE
SAGGY DOWN TO THE
FLOOR!
BUT ALL BOOBS ARE
PRECIOUS, SO LET'S
FIND A CURE!

About the Author....

Scott Clarke is an artist, writer and teaching artist hoping to
enlighten, inspire and entertain with his creativity.
Scott spends most of his time drawing,
writing and working as an art instructor
in addition to being a mentor through
diverse creative outreach programs.
He has a well received list of published books, assorted
collections of greeting cards and other commodities
featuring his creations. With few limits Scott
finds many outlets for his creative energy
coloring the world with love, light and laughter.
website www.scottclarkestudio.com
email scottclarkestudio@aol.com
facebook Scott Clarke
twitter @_scottclarke
instagram _scottclarke